Saint Michael in Peril of the Sea

Saint Michael in Peril of the Sea

JANICE FITZPATRICK SIMMONS

June 9, 2004

For Jim
at Salmon Summer Fest.

Janice Fitzpatrick Simmons

salmonpoetry

Published in 2009 by
Salmon Poetry
Cliffs of Moher, County Clare, Ireland
Website: www.salmonpoetry.com
Email: info@salmonpoetry.com

ISBN 978-1-907056-08-6

Cover artwork: *January Seascape* by Ian Gordon
Cover design & typesetting: Siobhán Hutson
Printed in England by imprint*digital*.net

Saint Michael in Peril of the Sea receives financial assistance from the Arts Council

To all the Students of The Poets' House
past and present

Acknowledgements

Acknowledgements are due to the following publications in which some of these poems were previously published:

"Penelope and The Suitors" and "Flycatcher" appeared in *Passages North*, Northern Michigan University.

"Wild Carrot" appeared in *Heliotrope*, A Journal of Poetry, New York.

"Lughnasa" appeared in *Salmon: A Journey of Poetry, 1981-2007* (Salmon Poetry, 2007)

Contents

I. Penelope On The Suitors

Penelope On The Suitors	13
Stasis	15
The Channel	16
Long Evenings	19
The Flow	20
Wild Carrot	21
The Nest in the Wind	23
The Beauty of Bog Fires	24
Car Crash	25
Light Bearers	26
Drift	27
The Hermit	28
Lughnasa	29
The Sound In His Head	30
The Poets' House	31
Finding Home	32
Waiting	33
The Colour of Autumn Leaves	34
Boundaries	35
The Find	36
Denial	37
Samhain	38
Flycatcher	39
View	40
Energy To Burn	41
Risk Taking	42
Observation of Birds	43

II. The Royal Canal

Locks   47
Celebrations   48
Swan Alone   49
Lost Things   50

III. Saint Michael In Peril of The Sea

Saint Michael In Peril of The Sea   53
All Souls' Day   54
Someday   55
Today   56
The Poets' House Again   57

I.

Penelope On The Suitors

Penelope On The Suitors

My house, when it started,
was full of the tokens of love—
a bird that flew and sang uncaged
with a song of a lark and of a woodthrush
warbling in its throat. One of the suitors—
it became such a frenzy of taking—took the bird
and when it flew straight home to me
there was no life left in the poor thing.

My son was small and I took to locking
myself away in the inner rooms
in what ceased to be my home.
Women friends and those who worked for me
took to gossip and sleeping with "the guests."
Guests! Assorted politicians, minor poets,
one good bard and a bunch of thieves,
God help me.

When I began to sort what had been taken
my mind seized on parlay and defense.
I knew I could weave and I wove.
Athena and Arachne came to me in dream.
There they taught me how I might weave a web
that would not end. Every night I wove
singing the secret chant until I counted
twenty years.

When I opened the door I did not know him
for he was a mature man in his middle prime.
If he was not the man I knew, still he was a husband.
He assessed the turmoil, caught my son in his embrace
and cleared the hall.

We got to know each other slow, and if the secret of our bed
was passed on or if indeed this is him, it does not matter.
You can hear the olive woods' high note, the bed singing:
Home is the sailor, home from the sea.
The suitors are gone and I am clear, clear of it.

Stasis

Cold summer of uncertain change,
of letting go, moving on
from where all is only memory of what we were.
No energy now to weed my garden,
no time left
to redd all up around my kitchen.

I have work to go to in another place
but my home has not sold yet.
Alienated the lawyers say.

As I walk Ballyness
water sounds the dry scrape of bone on rock,
of a hand cracking as it stretches its fingers out
reaching toward unknowns.

Time moves me on.
Ballyness sparkles still
its many hues of blue and white
and golden sands glow.
Work is elsewhere now
and I am packed to go.

The Channel

1.

My body rises with desire
that pulls me under and lifts me up

on the long strand as bright as a diamond
in a dark summer laden with mist and rain.

Three quarters the length on Magheraroarty
and we sit down to soak in sun, our growing affection,
the endless brightness of water, sand and sky.

O! our bodies gentled and tired,
work nearly done for the day,
always nearly done for the day.
We rest near marram, tide out,
a darkness floats on the water

between harbour and beach, nearly ominous
and then a dolphin and two others surface
as black as my black dress, breaking, breaking
turquoise and navy water, feeding
on the dark shoal of herring or lithe.

Where we lie your chest under my hand
is velvet and your heart is a wren
in the palm of my hand.

2.

You are readying yourself to leave,
you will distance between us as real
as your journey that will bring you to a German city,
into the arms of another.

How will it be for you there—
wine and beer outdoors, jazz in the afternoon
on a tree-lined street; a trip to mountains amid rampant
alpine flowers of late summer?

O, love it is still raining.
I have not walked the strand since that day.
I light a candle in my bedroom,
Work on bringing my house to order.

3.

When you return what will be left—
the leonids have played out their blue flame
in the heavens of August.
What will we know of each other;
will we walk again in early autumn
by the great strand of Magheraroarty?

I cannot tell, I do not predict, I don't know.
But here there is a place for us
for the complexities of love,
for its surprises that break and break again
the water of the harbour with the joy of dolphins
in the middle of a shoal of fish,
calling to each other across the water,
over the distance that separates them.

Long Evenings

If I asked him to come,
though spring has come
and new life lifts about him,
though we might smile and work
my weedy garden together, or leave it all
to walk the strand, the sunset strand,
the illuminant waves, the Brent geese
gathering before they leave,
still he would not come

though his love for me
is the love that belongs to Venus
rising over the dunes, is the pole star,
the one I fix on to define home,
is true to itself

he would not come to me
for he is caught so amid his history
of hotel and dinner, children and grandchildren,
protecting and providing,
of self denial.

So I walk the strand alone,
oyster catcher's embattled cries pierce me,
the evening star shines alone too above me,
and salmon find their way up the Ray.
It is spring, the pink and blue radiant water full of life
brings in the lengthening evenings of my absolute solitude.

The Flow

Larks above the dunes
hold in the bright air.
A hare hides still amid the marram grass;
there are marks that say sheep have
moved here some time earlier this day.

We are walking this spit of sand,
Atlantic waters northern summer turquoise
and dark blue-green shimmer in light
that shines with blazing intensity.

Another summer in and here we are
with more than we expected;
this walk, shelves of sand to shelter in
above the tide line in each other's arms.

Later stars will come out around us
and we will make our way to my bed;
all muscle and flesh, all desire
caught again in the full tide
of our bodies' language, making a music
of larks above dunes—the body
taking and giving what it needs.

Wild Carrot

The New England coast drifts by—
its moss colours, the deep gold of sea-oats
and sedge grass burnt by last years sun,
burning that part of my mind that
walks the beach with my father—
the wonder, still the wonder of sweet
earthiness in wild carrot. Who will remember
that beach walk but me—his hand picking
the green top and his asking me to taste?

Little clap-board harbour buildings and wooden docks,
the familiar shining water, small cypress on an outcrop island,
gold touched and distant from life
I've made elsewhere. Trees are a wonder
and the scenes flicker, fade from my seat
on Acela travelling New York to Providence.
The mobiles intrude and some talk incessantly,
but a man works across from me on his diary.

My partner smiles at me and at the diarist.
There is nothing that can hide the signs
of concentration—the mind working things,
here is a fellow practitioner. His wife is next to him
quiet, working too on needlepoint. She hands him
realtor's photos—ideal Vermont homes—white clap-board,
dark green doors and shutters on acres of land.
Breathe in the smell of cut grass,
close your eyes to see the leaves
of countless trees lift to the sun. And so, as with all
train journeys , to pass houses and towns is to walk
amid what might have been your life.

When the train pulls in I am on the Northwest Coast
of Ireland, pulling into Penn Station, meeting my brother-in-law

on a platform in Providence—where parting fell between us
like a shutter slamming shut on light.
I am hungry for home too—the high empty bog, early spring,
the day lengthening to a near midnight sun, my beautiful son;
my life where I've made it home—where love and loss are one.

The Nest in the Wind

The wind made the walking hard
and I was breathy before I climbed the dune
of Magheraroarty. O darling, o nest of curls,
o lover you push me. To where? Where are
we going; this good love, the breakers of autumn
water crashing in on the shore?

It is true, you walk toward me,
not even the angels deny us
and good looks down laughing at our play.

There is no looking back.
You taught me that. The sand
ghosts with the wind. O darling, o nest of curls,
you push me higher along the dunes of Magheraroarty
where God's voice is the sound of waves and wind
granting this brief space of privacy.

The Beauty of Bog Fires

The hills of evening are black
and lit by wild fires. It is beautiful
to watch the bright light spread against
the backdrop of hedges and measured fields;
my gorse watches—
beautiful the way the orange glow dies in one place

and lights in another; beautiful, how the stars
blink in a velvet- black dome above the fire
burning in darkness, the fire that must be put out
because nests and dens are burning
and flame has its own purpose
feeding on the air that gives life to small things

living amid branch and flower.
How close fire comes to barns and byres, how close to home.
I hear the engines coming. Soon the fire will be stopped,
the ground left singed, no sweet smelling whin
left to cover bare earth, no meadow sweet, no spikes of loosestrife.
Earth will take-in what remains—carbon, water, seed
to make something reborn from catastrophe.

Car Crash

In early autumn everything of regret seeps
with the rain into my heart.
There are tropical storms that blow
themselves out here as high wind.
The heavy downpour of my heart is
as high as the flood water of the falling
season. The sun that never came
is a ruin of what might have been.

The lawn chairs spilled over in the wind
last night and I called to you
but you will not hear my sadness
tearing from the trees with the chill winds.
Lover, I am not whole and we

are not one. A car crashed
at the back window of my bedroom,
its reckless speed could have spilled
my life onto the bedroom floor.

Light Bearers

There has been no summer.
The mists and damps have left
my middle-age bones achy in the morning.

I walk across the floor
hunched over until I straighten out.
Is it the weather or

the love I practice faith with?
Why faith at this late stage, faith
when I know that nothing prevents

loss, that as surely as I rise
a day will come that will separate me
from myself, my physical body.

I shower, dry my hair, put on my face,
and wonder about my steps toward you,
faltering, stiff, undeniably toward

what is at last the only act that matters:
Make use of the light while there is still time.

Drift

The Atlantic tides bring sand dollars in spring.
I take two fragile shells and bring one home to rest
on a windowsill below old lace, next to a blue glass bird.
The other shell I have given to one I love.

A thousand pin pricks on the shell form a star,
a symbol of hope cast up from deep water.
From my window I see the rain fall,
moving in waves southwest.

Clouds are a shadow passing over my mood.
When my son returns from shopping in town I remember
a pink freckled pebble and pull it from my pocket for him.
This is give and take, the sea coming in and pulling out.

I wonder when the one I love holds me again
how will it be? I close my eyes and see a hand outstretched
bearing a star, a shell, hope, a fragile thing.

The Hermit

The world has withdrawn and I am still
beside mountains. The lamp before me
is the passion of our bed and the future of my son—
the reasons I burn and care to go on.

My life stands before me—
a loaded gun—but words make faith
possible. Pebbles roll in and out with the tide;
their sounds are multitudes.

Angels come and go in cars.
No one on the strand where I am
closest to his presence and his absence,
no, not even a seal today

only the distant cries of curlew
and kittiwakes; the dusk coming down—
yellow neon lights on the horizon.

Lughnasa

For Gearóid MacLochlainn

I've got the end of summer blues.
I've got the end of summer moving on blues.
I've got the end of summer not enough money to buy clothes blues.
I've got the moving on, moving into rented accommodation blues.

I've got the blues
I've got the end of summer not knowing a soul blues.
I've got the moving on love in abeyance blues.
I've got the end of summer blues.
I've got the end of summer moving on leaving the graveside blues.

I've to the end of summer getting older blues.
I've got the blues, the weather howling,
storm engulfed, autumn coming blues.
There is nothing for it cause I have
the end of summer, love in abeyance blues.

I've got the blues, the monoglot, want to be on
a beach in France blues. An end of summer
miss the poets, moving on blues.

I've got the blues, I am playing Joni Mitchell's *Blue*,
I am sitting in my blue living room with end of summer,
the end of summer, moving on, getting older blues.

The Sound In His Head

At the kitchen table I sip coffee.
The turf fire makes the house warm
and my hand moves across the page
where I am singing a happy song to myself—
mother and son at either end of the house.

A heron overhead this fresh spring morning
blesses the day and my son—who moves determined
beyond his years, moves steadily
toward his father's unfulfilled desire
to make music the world will hear.
The whoosh of wings is his lifting voice,
his fingers reach for a sound
that is like the one in his head.

The Poets' House

The empty house,
no books or paintings
on the white walls,
no voices down the long hall,
no ghost voices,

no dog patters down stairs.
The sofa has no body
taking comfort there.
The house is empty and its stillness
puddles within the wall of my chest—
it's a hollow sound.

Finding Home

Two arms hold the Celtic Sea,
sea water rolls into Tramore.
Today the wind has brought large swells
and light swings very bright to very dark.

The strand and cliffs
are nothing like the strand and cliffs
of the northwest—lost to me now.
I get in the car and drive for city and campus
to do work I love. The meditation while I commute
is on the quality of light,
not so unlike the quality of light on Magheraroarty
though the sky is brighter more often here.

The weather is clearing, indigo and salmon clouds,
the red of the rising sun are on the water
as I round Cliff Road and make my way
to whatever lies ahead.

Waiting

Morning quayside,
waiting for you here,
for the storm of you.
Waiting under grey skies,
cold weather, traffic beginning
to tail off rush hour.

Pigeons peck at bits of rubbish.
The big ugly buildings
across the river ruin
any chance of a relieving view
to hills rising to a plateau.

A new family crisis
will pick at you
and I will offer
the little a friend can;
stay my speech
hold you hold me in place.

The Colour of Autumn Leaves

Here we are waking together
in a house where the river turns
into the sea. Snowy egrets,

cloud grey herons
pump their awkward wings
towards heaven, the last of autumn leaves
make a lover's sigh in light wind.

Our love is the colour of, autumn leaves,
haunts us into each other's arms
there to murmur and burn.

Boundaries

Four heron coming in
their wingspread full
flying low and graceful
on my horizon.

Another heron is in the water
one leg resting up on the other
in that fixed and familiar pose.
It is a mild day, it is quiet,
not quite spring,

I am walking where my heart is,
walking boundaries
where the Suir estuary
meets a wider sea on the margin
of winter, on the margin of spring,

caught by a pale grey sky,
caught by love I feel for him,
drawn here by the need for solace
from what I pull in from outside.

The Find

Grey of early dawn disappears
into pinks and blues over the blue grey water
that begins to shimmer as the first hint
of yellow reaches from the east

where I sit and look at the estuary,
a cup of coffee near my hand
at the table that is situated here to command
the view and give a proper perspective
on the unfolding day.

The cacophony of sea birds swells
over the oyster beds making a din—not music.
Egrets and herons poised reminding me
of Chinese paintings—
the ones with the golden light behind them.

I would like to sit at this table a long time—
watch estuary waters shimmer and birds hunt
the margins of sea and land.

Denial

I have been waiting
at the blank station—
no coffee shop, no place
that sells a little breakfast.
the train is always delayed
and that is my symbol
of you and me.

I am in a life of denial.
we are lovers,
I wear widow's weeds and talk
about him to fill in the gaps
between you and me.

Samhain

The lights have not yet come on in Duncannon.
Ben is away and it is dark night autumn calling in winter.
The sea is dark pewter, rolling liquid metal
into estuary shores. I shelter in a house amid trees

where the low slub of receding water breaks on sand and rock,
where the high sound of trees in wind and the rustle of dead leaves
is the earth's lament. I can hear the voices
of barren trees fading into sleep.

How sheltered I am from the winds that blow,
how exposed. Dark clouds in a gathering darkness
fly by. I must reach deep underneath to find my way
through empty nights toward spring.

Flycatcher

You came to me this morning.
Desire drove your will
and our love was urgent.
In the brightness of day
there was no pretence of tenderness.
I knew what you needed
and I gave it freely.

The flycatcher in the clematis at my door
feeds her brood;
it is a necessary thing
for her nature is to give.
Soon the young will fledge and depart.

When your car pulled out from the driveway
the bird sat—mouthful of flies—
on a dead bush. Her head's movement
checking what would watch and find her nest.

Nothing could stop my heart from breaking,
my ears thrumming with the sound of tires on gravel.

View

A window with the faintest outline of my reflection
and I reflect looking out at the brightest sky so blue—
orange clouds and pink on blue water—dawn's perfection.

I thole the present and all I have achieved.
My gaze is outward to Duncannon, the view
a village on the further shore; a shining whiteness believed

or half believed by me to be a symbol of hope and promise.
The closer view is the leaves turning colour, of blowing leaves
in mild autumn wind that shakes the plum tree to winter spareness.

Bees seek out pollen in the ivy, last of a rich season.
My son, a young man now, his hair newly cropped, his seriousness,
his humour all his own brings me coffee ready for action,

ready to move into his own life. Am I ready too?
This is not the last season, horizons blue and golden, new.

Energy To Burn

in memory of James Simmons

I walk by the sea: it has the power
to wash away years.
It is fierce with life.
Blue green waters thunder and foam
hurling down the long strand at Tramore.
Yesterday a small dolphin
flesh torn and gnawed,
lay dead on the strand.

Wary with life I understand
now why my mother would call me
away from that element that swept her
and two of my kindergarten sisters out a mile;
her powerful, desperate tread keeping them all afloat
until the coastguard lifted the three
from deadly cold west Atlantic waters

where I swam too.
I swam until brine burned tongue and lips.
I could fly in that element
and leapt in the waves and glided
ignoring the terror of sharks,
ignoring the power of the ocean tides and currents,
fierce in that water, as children must be fierce.

In the office my feet still tread sand,
I walk beside that element, my blood in the same salt balance
with storm turquoise of swelling water,
its white churned crash,
alive with energy to burn.

Risk Taking

Where am I now? Driving through flood water
terrified as the water pushes ahead of me
a wave that increases momentum; carries the car
through to the other side where I pull over
take a deep breath in relief. I made it through
but will take the high road home next time.

I was good at this once, younger,
unbowed by loss, unafraid of lack, a warrior
like all warriors carrying what they need within.
Funny though I wouldn't go back, not back.
I am impelled forward by time,
but by something else too—by desire.
So now is a time for structures and
frameworks of craft and institution.

Somehow I have made it home,
pull my car into its mooring by my little rented
cottage near the sea, open the gate,
follow the stone steps down,
down through the garden with angel, birdfeeder, bird bath,
watch dangerous water from my windows, from a safe distance.

Observation of Birds

The fat robin comes to my window looking for crumbs,
a heron whispers by on great wings. This is the edge,
where land meets a mingling of salt and sweet water.
I nest on the hill of sweet water and here offer solace
and attentions to my lover and care to my son
now a young man. Birds too are in their nests for it is spring again.

Amid the territorial birdsong of the woods in Woodstown
the wind makes a sound, the sound of a gently swaying Atlantic.
Birds, young man and lover rocked in the cradle of a nest,
taking for granted the balmy air, abundant food, sweet water—
imagining flight, yearning toward some other life.

II.

The Royal Canal

Locks

The worst fear I have
is travelling through a grave—
the dark in which somehow your eyes
still see the light. We came to the gates
and you left the barge with lock key,
to open those gates for me—

the gates held shut against me,
the gates where Odysseus
summoned his dead to presence.
And there I was at the gates middle aged,
driving Charon's boat across the Styx.
What a wild panic! The barge steering
itself against my will.

You were straining with the machinery
to let me through. How could I let you down?
Anger at my fear fed me now
so I mastered the barge, drove into the lock
and held there while the gates gonged shut behind me.

Celebrations

Thomastown Harbour mellow
warm spring evening on the Royal Canal
with you. Blackthorns and willow blossoming
on the banks. This the warmest spring that I remember.

A canal boat, you and me,
hard physical work—tired and rewarded
by experience. The small dark cered moorhens
in their nests; mooring sometimes *au sauvage*—in nature—
Thoreau and Walden Pond—this journal
and notes of how I love you.

The dawn chorus of birds is many voiced,
so many voices for us to hear and hear again.
Here is our journey with a purpose.
You and I on the canal that moves on,
moves slowly toward you and slowly toward me.

Swan Alone

A swan without a mate
followed the barge along the canal.
She was a harbinger
of what it is to live without,
for now she loved the barge
and followed its movements.

Following first from a distance and behind
I watched the growing light gather round
her whiteness. Then in an ecstasy of wings
she passed low over the boat—
her curving body and the audible
beat of wings ten feet above me. Me the girl inside
was caught by tears for you my lost mate.
And here I was on a barge with a man I love

who leaves me mostly on my own
but not now coming from Westmeath's
Thomastown, through Hyde Park,
the Cappagh Bog. The swan floated in the light
of a rising clay-red sun burning
the frost to a ghosting mist leading us on
to The Hill of Down and then rising she was gone,
returned to her own mysteries.

Lost Things

Shimmering pink sea water
in the sand flats and out further
tractors, oyster gatherers bending
to their cold work—a little cold

in this room too, so the children
not children build me a fire
while I watch the sun go down
thinking about lost things
and the future with or without you.

III.

Saint Michael In Peril of The Sea

Saint Michael In Peril of The Sea

Hot day in Brittany on this busman's bluemoon holiday
in the pink granite longière of our first vacation
abroad together. Bright flowers in bloom, geranium and stock,
rose and peony abundant as our yearning, alive together
in the forest of Broceliande where Viviane and Merlin
lie with each other hidden from the eyes of men
waiting til they are called to serve again.

We make a pilgrimage
to a church where I watch the roof's stone guttering
of gargoyles, monkeys pouring water
from their granite mouths. The God of imagination
and earth's magic are alive here. Inside the ceiling
of the chapel is latticed with carved angels who wing
their way to God. He hold his son at Loc Envel;
symbol of my one belief—
that God is love.

I am a devotee of St. Michael too, so you take me
to St. Michel en Grève where Arthur killed the dragon,
where St. Michael touched earth and began his race
with Lucifer for possession of Mount Tombe.
Christianity planted its roots in rock
where Merlin buried the sun after the fall
of the round table and here now I climb
the ancient streets of Mont St. Michel
to the cathedral on Milton's guarded Mount
—*Look Homeward Angel now...*

I wonder at the austere light of the cloisters
its heart soaring new view of the bay where surprised
I remember penitents who suffered the knife's edge here—
my quick intake of breath followed by letting it go.
You reach for my hand—the sure human connection
now blessed and open, our gaze reaching outward and up.

All Souls' Day

Lost on roads not known
I crossed the bridge at The Hill of Down
and wept for us. I calmed myself
with a cup of coffee in the pub that to my suprise
banked the Royal Canal where we docked
the canal boat last spring. I hold on to the familiar
as swans float by, their reflection bright on the dark surface.
My mind brims with this flood water:

the sun on the deck of an Easter boat,
the walk up Abbey steps on Mont St. Michel,
the carved ceiling of a chapel at Loc Envel,
the white sand of Magheraroarty,
how each time we meet our bodies tell us
what your mind can't hear.

Someday

All you bring with you is your childhood faith
in love, its fragile fallible nature, your strength
that will guide you as you travel—
you will be asked to hold on and to
let go. Someday you will hold the one you love
in your arms and you will tell him that he can die,
that he was a great man.

Maybe you will put on music that he loved
and your son will be on the bed beside him
learning loss and the depth of love that wells
from who knows where.

Your path is still before you, and say it leads you
onto the great strand at Magheraroarty with a friend;
the day is bright and the water bright in storm winds,
Inisboffin bright then dark under swift clouds—

and you know your nature is to reach for another,
is to love as best you can. It's a risk,
you know it because the voices of the dead,
the voices of past love have reached a crescendo in the storm
but here it is and maybe wrong-headed—
you reach your hand out and he touches and holds.

Today

the last flame of summer flowers—montbretia
in gardens, wild in hedges, burning with orange fire
spending itself. Down the long road from home
the flowers ornate candelabras lead me through
morning by mountains, afternoon amid grey-eyed lakes.
I travel the rolling midlands; tongues of flame around
cairns and fairy forts—lost history.   The divided self
spends its energy on harvest, the golden fields ploughed
and ordered, the city of work waiting with a small rented
cottage by the sea where I count up the passing hours—
time burning itself out by meanings lost, by wanderings.

The Poets' House Again

I didn't sell the house—
my heart is in
a ring of mountains round bays of white sands,
I have re-made it now my family home.
Ghosts are welcome, the claws of the family dog,
the clump of my husband's feet in the library.

My golden bedroom is not so lonely—
a beloved presses himself toward me.
My son returns to his family home
my step-daughter happy to come and see
the new kitchen, hear the old creaking of the doors.
There are books on shelves again, the pictures hung,
rooms transformed from public space to private.

I look forward to the blossoming
of the clematis where the flycatcher nests,
to the acrobatics of mating swallows,
to the fledglings first flight, to my lover's return.
I have learned to live with compromise,
travelling the length of Northwest, Southeast,
counting the time by its intensity.